Schleswig-Holstein

Dieter Steffen · Uwe Paulsen

Schleswig-Holstein

Wachholtz Verlag

Vorwort

Schleswig-Holstein

Schleswig-Holstein ist das nördlichste Land der Bundesrepublik Deutschland.

Durch seine Abgrenzung im Osten und Westen durch die Meere und im Süden durch die Elbe erscheint Schleswig-Holstein als einheitliches geographisches Gebilde mit natürlichen Grenzen. Nur in Richtung Norden wurde erst 1920 nach einer Volksabstimmung die jetzt gültige Grenze zum Nachbarland Dänemark gezogen. So deutlich diese Einheit Schleswig-Holsteins auf der Karte zu erkennen ist, so vielfältig ist dieser Raum doch in sich gestaltet. Der unterschiedliche Charakter von Marsch, Geest und Jungmoränenland kennzeichnen das Land ebenso wie die flache Nordseeküste mit ihren vorgelagerten Watten, Halligen und Inseln und die Ostseeküste mit ihren Steilufern und tief ins Land einschneidenden Förden.

Von besonderer Bedeutung für seine Entwicklung und für eine wechselhafte Landesgeschichte ist die geographische Lage Schleswig-Holsteins als Landbrücke zwischen Mittel- und Nordeuropa. Sie diente den Völkerwanderungen, dem Kulturaustausch zwischen Mitteleuropa und Skandinavien und dem Fernhandel. Zur Überwindung der Landbarre nutzte man früh Wasserwege, die gemeinsam mit kurzen Landstrecken die beiden Meere miteinander verbanden. Besonders an der Ostseeküste entstanden bedeutsame Zentren des Handels mit den Ostseestaaten. Die Hansestadt Lübeck zeugt noch immer von der Bedeutung. Ein wesentlicher Güteraustausch wird heute durch den Nord-Ostsee-Kanal geführt, der zu den wichtigsten Seeschiffahrtskanälen der Welt zählt.

Etwa 2,7 Millionen Menschen leben heute in diesem Land, in dem es nur zwei Großstädte gibt: Kiel, die Landeshauptstadt und Lübeck, die alte Hansestadt. Fischerei und Landwirtschaft sind die ältesten Wirtschaftszweige und noch Dreiviertel der Landesfläche wird landwirtschaftlich genutzt. Schleswig-Holstein weist heute jedoch eine sehr breitgefächerte Wirtschaftsstruktur auf und es arbeiten mittlerweile mehr Menschen in der Computerindustrie als in der Landwirtschaft. Es ist für viele Unternehmen zum attraktiven Industrie- und Dienstleistungsstandort geworden.

Besondere Bedeutung kommt dem Fremdenverkehr zu, der schon eine lange Tradition in diesem Lande hat. Viele Besucher werden jährlich von den Nord- und Ostseebädern angezogen, aber auch das Binnenland lockt mit vielen attraktiven Zielen.

Die geologische Dreigliederung des Landes - im Osten das seenreiche, fruchtbare Hügelland, im Mittelstreifen die Geest mit ihren mageren Böden und im Westen das fruchtbare, vom Meer abgelagerte und häufig vom Hochwasser gefährdete Marschland mit seinen vorgelagerten Inseln und Halligen - soll uns in ihrer Reihenfolge die Bildreise durch das Land und seine Städte vorgeben.

6

Foreword

Schleswig-Holstein

Schleswig-Holstein is the most northerly state of the German Federal Republic. Its borders to the east and west are formed by the Baltic and the North Sea and to the south by the river Elbe, altogether conveying the impression of a geographical landmass completely intact within natural borders. Only to the north, after the plebiscite in 1920 was the border with Denmark finally and permanently defined. Homogenous and intact as Schleswig-Holstein appears on the map, there are nevertheless marked obvious geographical differences within this region. The natural, contrasting features consisting of marshland, sandy moorland and undulating moraine landscape are particularly characteristic, as are the low-lying North Sea coastal shore areas with their offshore and mudflats, large and tiny islands (Halligen) as well as the Baltic coast with its cliffs and sharply indenting fjords cutting deeply into the land.

Its geographical position has greatly influenced the varied history of this region and its development as a land bridge between central and northern Europe. This has facilitated the migration of peoples and cultural exchanges with central Europe and Scandinavia as well as foreign trade. To overcome the land barrier in the early days, use was made of waterways, which together with short land routes, connected both seas. On the Baltic coast especially, important trade centres came into being to serve the trade with the Baltic states. The Hanseatic city of Lübeck even today is of considerable importance as a centre of commerce. A considerable flow of goods is still transported via the Kiel Canal, one of the world's most important waterways.

Today, approximately 2.7 million people live in Schleswig-Holstein which has only two major cities: Kiel, the state capital and Lübeck, the old Hanseatic port.

Fishing and agriculture are the oldest branches of industry, threequarters of the total land area is still used for agriculture. The economic structure of Schleswig-Holstein is, however, broadly based. There are for instance more people employed in the computer industry than in agriculture. For many firms involved in the service and manufacturing industries it has become an attractive location.

Tourism has had a long tradition and plays a vital role in this region. The seaside resorts on the North Sea and Baltic coasts are an annual attraction for many holidaymakers. The interior, too has much to offer the visitor.

The three-part geological division of Schleswig-Holstein i.e. the fertile hill country in the east with its many lakes, the central area with its sandy moorlands and infertile soil, the western area with its fertile marshland of silt deposited by the sea, often endangered by high tides, and its offshore islands and islets (Halligen), form the basis in this order for our journey in pictures throughout this region including its cities and towns.

Mölln ist ein liebevoll gepflegtes Städtchen, das in der Ansicht durch den hohen Kirchenhügel mit St. Nikolai geprägt ist. Schon im 13. Jahrhundert war Mölln eine attraktive Haltestelle an der vielbefahrenen Salzstraße, die von Lüneburg nach Lübeck führte. Bis heute hat es im Stadtkern seinen mittelalterlichen Charakter bewahrt. An der hohen Stützmauer des Kirchhofes sitzt das Wahrzeichen der Stadt, Till Eulenspiegel, ein bekannter Narr, der der Legende nach 1350 dort gestorben sein soll.

Mölln is a lovingly cared-for small town dominated by the high hill on which stands the church of St. Nicholas. As early as the 13th century it provided an attractive stop on the much traversed saltroad from Lüneburg to Lübeck. Fortunately, the medieval character of the town centre still exists. On the high retaining wall of the churchyard can be seen the statue of Till Eulenspiegel, world-famous jester and symbol of the town, who according to legend died here sometime after the year 1350.

Ratzeburg ist wegen seiner reiz- vollen Insellage und umgeben vom Naturpark Lauenburgische Seen ein Mittelpunkt des Ruder- und Angelsports und Ziel vieler Be- sucher. Der romanische Dom, im 12. Jahrhundert unter Heinrich dem Löwen gebaut, gehört zu den ersten monumentalen Backstein- bauten im Lande. Barlach, der in Ratzeburg lebte, schuf die Skulptur „Der Bettler" für den Klosterhof.

Ratzeburg in its attractive island setting, surrounded by the Nature Park Lauenburgische Seen is a rowing and fishing sports centre as well as a magnet for many visitors. Its 12th century Norman cathedral built by Henry the Lion is one of the most notable red-brick monumental edifices in Schleswig-Holstein. The artist Ernst Barlach, who lived in Ratzeburg, created the sculpture "The Beggar", seen in the cloister yard.

Die Entwicklung von Bad Oldesloe wurde entscheidend beeinflußt durch die Funktion als Umschlagsplatz auf dem Transitweg Lübeck-Hamburg und später durch die Salzgewinnung. Die Innenstadt ist geprägt durch den mittelalterlichen Altstadtkern, der von den Flüssen Trave und Bresse umschlossen wird. Alte Bausubstanz und moderne Architektur stehen am Stadthaus in reizvollem Kontrast.

The decisive and influencing factor in the development of Bad Oldesloe was its function as a centre of commerce on the transit trade route Lübeck - Hamburg, together with salt-mining at a later stage. The town centre is dominated by the medieval old quarter surrounded by the rivers Trave and Bresse. Old and modern architecture near the Stadthaus forms an attractive contrast.

Das bekannte Wahrzeichen der Kreisstadt Bad Segeberg ist der Kalkberg, der bis ins 17. Jahrhundert eine bedeutende landesherrliche Burg trug. Im Laufe von Jahrhunderten haben die Segeberger ihren Burgfelsen um mindestens 20 m abgebaut und das begehrte Baumaterial verkauft. Heute mißt er nur noch 90 Meter. Vor der Felsruine bietet eine Freilichtbühne Platz für 10.000 Besucher, die in jeden Sommer die beliebten Karl-May-Festspiele besuchen. Der historische Kern ist ebenso Anziehungspunkt wie ein weit über die Region bekanntes Möbelhaus.

The well-known landmark of the district town Bad Segeberg is the Kalkberg which well into the 17th century was surmounted by a dominating castle. During the following centuries the inhabitants of the town reduced the height of the castle rock by at least 20 metres by selling the chalk as a much-desired building material. Today it measures only 90 metres in height. What remains of the rock serves as a backdrop to the open air theatre for 10,000 visitors, who every summer come to see the popular Karl May Festival. The historical centre of the town is as much an attraction as the well-known furniture store.

Lübeck, die bedeutende Hansestadt, wurde bereits im Jahre 1143
gegründet und entwickelte sich
wegen der verkehrsgünstigen Lage
schnell zu einem wichtigen und
wohlhabenden Handelsort, der
Stützpunkte im gesamten Ostsee-
raum unterhielt. Noch heute ist das
ehrwürdige Stadtbild erhalten und
von der UNESCO als Weltkultur-
erbe anerkannt. Das Holstentor,
Rest einer Befestigungsanlage, ist
wohl die bekannteste Sehenswür-
digkeit der Stadt. Heute hat sich
um Lübeck herum eine breitgefächerte und leistungsfähige Industrie etabliert. Weltweit bekannt ist
das hier hergestellte Marzipan.

*Lübeck, the famous Hanseatic city,
founded in 1143, largely because
of its convenient position, soon
became one of the most important
and prosperous centres of trade
with footholds in the whole of the
Baltic region. Its dignified
townscape has been preserved for
posterity and has been designated
a world cultural heritage by the
UNESCO. The Holstentor, part of
the original fortified wall, is indeed
the most famous attraction of the
city. Around the city varied and
productive industries have been
established. The locally produced
marzipan is of world-wide fame.*

Lübeck war die Heimatstadt von Thomas Mann, der in seinem Roman Buddenbrooks die großbürgerlichen Verhältnisse schildert, in denen er aufwuchs. Das Haus, in dem große Teile des Romans spielen, ist erhalten und kann besichtigt werden.

Lübeck was the home town of Thomas Mann who in his novel "Buddenbrooks" paints a vivid picture of the patrician way of life in which he grew up. The house in which many of the events described in the novel took place, has been preserved as a museum and can be visited.

Ein Spaziergang durch die Straßen
Lübecks läßt noch immer den
Glanz der Hanse spüren.

One has only to stroll through the
streets of Lübeck to sense the
pervading atmosphere of the
Hanseatic League.

Travemünde zählt zu den ältesten Seebädern und wirkt heute noch durch seine mondäne Ausstrahlung anziehend auf die Besucher. Seit der Öffnung der innerdeutschen Grenze sind den Besuchern auch die weiten Strände der Ostseite offen. Auf dem Priwall liegt zur Besichtigung das ehemalige Segelschulschiff „Passat".

Travemünde, one of the oldest seaside resorts, still attracts visitors with its chic and modern ambience. Since the opening of the border between the two Germanies, visitors have access to the broad beaches of the Eastern part. The former training ship "Passat" can be visited on the Priwall.

Seit dem Aufkommen der Dampf-
schiffe ist der Travemünder Hafen
bedeutender Ausgangspunkt für
den Fährverkehr nach Dänemark,
Schweden und Finnland. Der alte
Leuchtturm ist schon lange nicht
mehr in Betrieb. Seine Aufgabe
übernahm das weitaus höhere
Maritim-Hotel, denn von dort
werden heute die Leuchtsignale
zur Orientierung der Seefahrer
ausgesendet.

*Since the advent of the steamship
the port of Travemünde has
become an important point of
departure for the ferry traffic to
Denmark, Sweden and Finland.
For many years the old lighthouse
has been out of use. Its function
has now been taken over by the
much taller Maritim-Hotel, from
where light signals are transmitted
to guide shipping.*

Neustadt ist eine alte Fischer- und Hafenstadt, deren Plananlage mit einem großen viereckigen Marktplatz in der Mitte erhalten ist. Der Pagodenspeicher an der nahegelegenen Hafenbrücke wurde 1828 erbaut und diente fortan, das Korn zu speichern. Im Hafen zeigt sich im Sommer ein buntes Bild durch die dort festmachenden Fischerboote und Sportschiffe.

Neustadt, an old fishing and harbour town, has a large square market place in the centre, preserved as part of its original layout. A pagoda-shaped storehouse, built in 1828 close to the harbour bridge, has since then served as a grain warehouse. In the summer the harbour presents a colourful scene with its moored fishing boats and leisure sailing craft.

In den Sommermonaten hat das Kulturleben in Schleswig-Holstein eine ganz besondere Attraktion. Wie hier auf Gut Hasselburg zieht es Tausende zu den Musikveranstaltungen auf's Land.
Das 1986 durch Justus Frantz ins Leben gerufene „Schleswig-Holstein Musik Festival" hat längst die Bedeutung eines internationalen Festivals erreicht.

During the summer months the cultural scene in Schleswig-Holstein is of special importance. Thousands of concertgoers are attracted to the musical events in rural surroundings as shown here on the Hasselburg estate. The Schleswig-Holstein Music Festival founded by Justus Frantz in 1986 is now of international significance.

Es sind nicht nur die Konzertsäle des Landes, in denen sowohl namhafte Künstler als auch der künstlerische Nachwuchs aus aller Welt auftreten, sondern ebenso Kirchen, Gutshäuser, Schlösser, Reithallen und Scheunen. Auch dies trägt zum besonderen Reiz des Festivals bei.

Well-known and young up-and-coming musicians from all over the world perform not only in concert halls, but also in churches, manor houses, castles, riding halls and barns, all adding a special charm to the events.

Erst mit dem Bau der Fehmarn-
sundbrücke 1962 wurde die Insel
Fehmarn mit dem Festland verbunden. Die Vogelfluglinie als Verkehrs-
anbindung nach Skandinavien und
die Errichtung eines großen Ferien-
zentrums haben die Insel entscheidend beeinflußt.

*In 1962 with the construction of a
bridge across the Fehmarn Sound
the island of Fehmarn was finally
linked to the mainland. The
"Vogelfluglinie" (direct line)
providing a traffic link to
Scandinavia together with the
building of a large holiday centre
have greatly affected the island's
importance.*

Fehmarn ist die größte Insel Schleswig-Holsteins und von abwechslungsreicher Küstenvielfalt. Vom Klima eindeutig bevorteilt, weist sie überdurchschnittlich mehr Sonnenstunden und weniger Niederschläge auf als der Durchschnitt des Landes. Das hat schon sehr früh die Badegäste angelockt.

Fehmarn, the largest island in Schleswig-Holstein, has a rich and varied coastline. Blessed with an advantageous climate, the island boasts more than the average number of sunshine hours and less rainfall than is usual in this region, an incentive for holidaymakers to come here earlier in the season.

Eutin, die ehemals fürstbischöfliche Residenz, ist eine malerische, alte Stadt mit sehr viel Charme. Inmitten einer anmutigen Seenlandschaft und umgeben von einem der großartigsten Landschaftsparks Schleswig-Holsteins ist diese Stadt ein attraktives Ziel vieler Besucher. Es lohnt ein Spaziergang durch die Rosenstadt, über den Markt und vorbei an den liebevoll erhaltenen Häusern.

Eutin, former prince-bishop's residence, is a picturesque, charming old town, set amidst a lovely lake landscape and surrounded by one of the most beautiful nature parks in Schleswig-Holstein, making it an attractive destination for many visitors. A stroll across the market square, through the town with its beautifully restored old houses of character and famed for its roses, is a pleasure at all times.

Ende des 18. Jahrhunderts erlebte die Stadt ihre kulturelle Blüte. Die Eutiner tun viel dafür, das geistig-kulturelle Erbe der Vergangenheit lebendig zu halten.

The town reached its cultural peak at the end of the 18th century. Today, however, the people of Eutin do much to preserve the historical and cultural heritage of the past.

Eine Besichtigung des renovierten Schlosses mit dem angrenzenden, in Stil englischer Landschaftsgärten angelegten Schloßpark ist ebenso lohnend wie ein Besuch der sommerlichen Aufführung der Werke von Carl Maria von Weber auf der Freilichtbühne am See.

A tour of the baroque castle and its grounds laid out in the style of an English landscape garden are also focal points of interest and attraction. The summer performances of works by Carl Maria von Weber in the open air theatre adjacent to the lake are an added attraction here.

Die Holsteinische Schweiz bietet Ruhe und Entspannung. Besonders schön ist sie zur Zeit der Rapsblüte mit dem typischen Schleswig-Holstein Himmel.

Pferdezucht hat in der Holsteinischen Schweiz Tradition. Die Zucht, die aus diesen Gestüten kommt, ist im nationalen und internationalen Reitsport von Bedeutung. Auch die Holsteiner Kühe haben es zu weltweiter Bekanntheit gebracht.

The Holsteinische Schweiz
presents an environment of peace
and relaxation. The season of the
flowering rape fields viewed
against a background of a typical
Schleswig-Holstein sky is a
panorama of outstanding natural
beauty.
Horse breeding is a tradition in the
Holsteinische Schweiz. The various
breeds resulting from these stud
farms have gained recognition in
the national and international field
of equestrian sports. Holstein cattle
too, have achieved their own
world-wide fame.

Im Herzen der Holsteinischen Schweiz und unmittelbar am großen Plöner See liegt der Luftkurort Plön. Ein Erholungszentrum, das viele Möglichkeiten des Wander- und Wassersports bietet.

The health resort of Plön is situated in the heart of the Holsteinische Schweiz on the edge of the large lake. As a holiday centre Plön offers many opportunities for both walking and water sports.

Das Plöner Schloß ist ein Wahrzeichen der Stadt. Das dreiflügelige Schloß aus dem 17. Jahrhundert diente in der Kaiserzeit als Kadettenanstalt und beherbergt nun ein staatliches Internat. Besonders imposant wirkt es, wenn man es während einer der beliebten Seenfahrten vom Dampfer aus betrachtet.

Plön Castle is the landmark of the town. This 17th century edifice, built in three wings, served during the reign of the emperors as a school for officer cadets and is now a state-owned boarding school. An imposing sight when viewed from one of the pleasure boats during a popular lake trip.

Im Kreis Plön stehen viele der Herrenhäuser des Landes. Sie waren einst Mittelpunkt der Höfe. Mit ihren mächtigen Scheunen und Stallungen gehörten sie zu den großen Gütern des Landes. Die heutigen Besitzer bemühen sich sehr, das Erbe der einst berühmten Adelskultur in Schleswig-Holstein zu erhalten. Gut Panker ist dafür ein hervorragendes Beispiel.

Many of the region's stately homes are to be found in the Plön area. They were once the centre of aristocratic courtly life. With their enormous barns and stables they number amongst the large estates of the region. Their present owners endeavour to maintain the heritage of the once renowned way of life of the nobility in Schleswig-Holstein. The Panker estate is an excellent example of this.

Vom Aussichtsturm Hessenstein, der nahe dem Gut liegt, hat man bei schönem Wetter einen großartigen Ausblick bis zu den dänischen Inseln.

On a fine day, from the observation tower Hessenstein, close to the Panker estate, one can see as far as the Danish islands.

Laboe liegt am Ausgang der Kieler Förde. Das Marine-Ehrenmal, in Form eines Schiffsstevens gebaut, überragt das Ostseebad. Wer die 85m hohe Aussichtsplattform erklimmt, hat einen weiten Blick über Meer und Land. Der Hafen von Laboe ist jährlich das Ziel einer Oldtimer-Regatta, zu der sich die schönsten Segelyachten einfinden.

Laboe is situated at the mouth of the Kieler Förde. Standing high above this Baltic resort is the naval memorial in the shape of a ship's stern-post. Those who climb the 85 m high observation platform, have a wonderful view over land and sea. The harbour of Laboe is the finishing post of the annual oldtimer regatta, when many of the most beautiful sailing yachts arrive and are to be seen.

Kiel, die Landeshaupstadt, liegt beiderseits der Innenförde. Schon seit 1665 Universitätsstadt, entwickelte sie sich erst mit der Bestimmung zum Flottenstützpunkt von der kleinen mittelalterlichen Stadt zur Marine- und Werftstadt von großstädtischem Ausmaß.

Kiel, the state capital, is situated on both banks of the inner Förde. A university town since 1665 which later became a naval base and has since grown from a small medieval town to a large city with a naval and shipyard presence.

Es waren Matrosen der in Kiel stationierten Kriegsschiffe, die 1918 Novemberrevolution auslösten. Großflächige Luftkriegszerstörungen im Zweiten Weltkrieg machten einen wesentlichen Neuaufbau der Stadt erforderlich. Der Rathausturm überragt die Innenstadt, die mit Fußgängerzonen und einem breitgefächerten Einzelhandel zu einem beliebten Einkaufszentrum für das gesamte Umland, aber auch für die zahlreichen skandinavischen Touristen wurde.

The November revolution in 1918 was set in motion by sailors of the warships stationed in Kiel. After World War II extensive rebuilding of the town was necessary as a result of the large areas of the city destroyed during air raids. The town centre, dominated by the tower of the town hall, together with its pedestrian shopping precincts and a wide range of retail shops has become a popular shopping venue, both for residents of the surrounding areas as well as for the numerous Scandinavian tourists.

Direkt an der Förde liegt das Landeshaus. Es ist Sitz der Landesregierung und des Schleswig-Holsteinischen Landtags. Hier beginnt Kiels schöne Uferpromenade, die „Kiellinie", die zur „Kieler Woche" Tausende von Besuchern anlockt.

The state government building is situated directly alongside the Förde. It is the home of the Schleswig-Holstein state government and state parliament. It is also the start of the beautiful Förde promenade called the "Kiellinie", an attraction during the "Kieler Woche" for thousands of visitors.

Die „Kieler Woche", weit über die Landesgrenzen bekannt, ist eine der größten Segelsportveranstaltungen der Welt. 22 Bootsklassen wetteifern auf den Regattafeldern in der Kieler Förde.

The "Kieler Woche" is one of the world's largest sailing sports events, well-known outside Schleswig-Holstein. Twenty-two classes of boats compete in regatta events that take place in the Kieler Förde.

Der Nord-Ostsee-Kanal, 1895 ein-
geweiht, zählt zu den meistbefah-
renen künstlichen Wasserstraßen
der Welt. Durch großangelegte
Schleusen in Kiel-Holtenau ge-
langen Schiffe bis zu 9,5m Tief-
gang in den Kanal und vermeiden
so den weiten Weg durch den
Großen Belt um Dänemark.

*The Kiel Canal was officially
opened in 1895 and ranks as one
of the most used man-made
waterways in the world. The
especially large locks in Kiel-
Holtenau enable ships of up to
9.5 m draught to enter the canal
and so avoid the roundabout route
through the Great Belt near
Denmark.*

Das Herrenhaus Schierensee wurde
Ende des 18. Jahrhunderts aus ro-
tem Backstein, dem traditionellen
norddeutschen Baumaterial, errich-
tet. Als eines der stattlichsten
Herrenhäuser wurde es von dem
Verleger Axel Springer mit großem
Aufwand renoviert. Durch seine
abgeschirmte Lage wird es von der
Straße her kaum wahrgenommen.

*The manor house of Schierensee
was built from red brick, the
traditional north German building
material, at the end of the 18th
century. One of the most imposing
manor houses of this region, it was
restored at great expense by the
publisher Axel Springer. Its
secluded position makes it hardly
noticeable from the road.*

Das Herrenhaus Emkendorf liegt im Naturschutzpark Westensee und wird heute privat genutzt. Der klassizistische Bau galt einst als Mittelpunkt des kulturellen Lebens in Schleswig-Holstein.

The manor house of Emkendorf, situated in the nature reserve Westensee, is now a private residence. Built in the classical style, it was once the centre of cultural life in Schleswig-Holstein.

Im 14. und 15. Jahrhundert sollen die Schiffe der Seeräuber von Eckernförde abgelegt haben. Heute drängen die Menschen zum Fischmarkt im Hafen, um dort Hering, Dorsch und Butt zu kaufen. Fischveredlung hat in der Stadt Tradition. Wer durch die gemütliche Fußgängerzone schlendert, landet unweigerlich am Hafen, wo der runde Getreidesilo steht.

During the 14th and 15th centuries according to legend pirate ships set off from Eckernförde. Now people head for the fish market in the harbour to buy herring, cod and flounder. Fish processing too, is an established tradition in the town. A stroll through the inviting pedestrian precinct leads one inevitably to the attractive harbour dominated by the large circular grain silo.

Über die hölzerne Klappbrücke gelangt man auf die andere Hafenseite. 1872 wurde sie anläßlich einer Sturmflut von Pionieren angelegt und blieb bis heute erhalten.

The opposite side of the harbour is reached via a wooden bridge. Constructed in 1872 by pioneers during a flood, it is still very much in use today.

Jahrhundertelang war Damp ein kleines, verschlafenes Dorf. Das änderte sich, als in den siebziger Jahren das Ferienzentrum „Damp 2000" erbaut wurde.
Der verkehrsberuhigte Ferienpark bietet nicht nur Urlaubern Erholung, sondern auch den vielen Patienten der Rehabilitations- und Ostseeklinik.

For hundreds of years Damp was a sleepy little village. All this changed when in the seventies the holiday centre "Damp 2000" was built. This holiday centre, largely traffic-free, offers relaxation not only to the holidaymakers but also to patients of the Rehabilitation/Baltic Sea Clinic.

Haithabu war einst der wichtigste mittelalterliche Umschlagplatz an der Ostsee. Nach seiner Zerstörung gründete man am Nordufer der Schlei Schleswig, die älteste Stadt Schleswig-Holsteins.
Der St. Petri Dom zeugt als eines der bedeutendsten Baudenkmale von der Bedeutung dieser Stadt. Die größte Schloßanlage des Landes befindet sich ebenfalls in Schleswig: Schloß Gottorf. Ein

prächtiges Renaissanceschloß, in dessen Räumen heute die Landesmuseen vereinigt sind. Die Ausstellungen von beachtlichen vorgeschichtlichen Funden bis hin zur zeitgenössischen Kunst sind einzigartig.

Haithabu was once the most important medieval trading place on the Baltic. After its destruction it became the site of Schleswig-Holstein's oldest town, Schleswig, founded on the northbank of the river Schlei. St. Peter's Cathedral, one of the most impressive historical monuments here, is indicative of the importance of this town. Schloss Gottorf, the largest castle in Schleswig-Holstein, is to

Im Haithabumuseum, das unter anderem ein mehr als 1000 Jahre altes Schiff zeigt, wird die Zeit der Wikinger lebendig.

The period of the Vikings is brought to life in the Museum of Haithabu where amongst other items a thousand-year old ship can be seen.

be found on the outskirts of Schleswig. A splendid complex of the Renaissance period, it houses the state's museums. Unique exhibitions ranging from notable pre-historic finds to the contemporary art are a regular feature here.

Die in die Schleilandschaft einge-
betteten Fischersiedlungen sind
von idyllischer Ausstrahlung. Der
Holm in Schleswig oder Arnis, die
kleinste Stadt Deutschlands, haben
ihren ursprünglichen Charakter
gewahrt. In Kappeln wird noch
heute mit der mittelalterlichen
Methode der Heringszäune der
Fischfang ausgeübt.

*The fishing communities on the
Schlei impart an idyllic charm.
Holm in Schleswig and Arnis, the
smallest town in Germany, have
retained their original character.
Today in Kappeln, fish is still
caught using the old medieval
method of herring fences.*

Rum begründete Flensburgs Ruhm. Bereits Ende des 18. Jahrhunderts bekamen die Flensburger Kaufleute von Westindien den zur Rumherstellung notwendigen Rohrzucker und noch bis heute haben die Weiterverarbeitung und Herstellung von Spirituosen und Bier ihre Tradition behalten. Das Nordertor als Zeugnis einer mittelalterlichen Befestigungsanlage steht am Rande der restaurierten Altstadt.

Rum has long been the basis of Flensburg's fame and fortune. At the end of the 18th century Flensburg's merchants received the raw cane sugar for the making of rum from the West Indies. Up to the present day the tradition of making spirits and beer has continued. The Northern Gate on the edge of the restored old part of the town is a relic of the medieval fortifications.

Einst größte Handelsstadt der Dänen, übt Flensburg heute eine wichtige Funktion als Grenzhandelsstadt aus. Die Stadt selbst und ihre reizvolle landschaftliche Lage sorgen für vielfältige Anziehungspunkte.

Formerly the largest Danish trading town, Flensburg now plays an important role as a border commercial centre. The town itself and its beautiful surrounding countryside is an attraction for many visitors.

Das Wasserschloß von Glücksburg, nicht weit entfernt an der Flensburger Förde gelegen, spiegelt sich im aufgestauten See. Das Schloß war herzögliche Residenz und im 19. Jahrhundert Sitz der Könige von Dänemark. Überregional bekannt ist die renommierte Hanseatische Yachtschule.

The castle of Glücksburg, not far from the Flensburger Förde, whose reflection can be seen in the still waters of the moat, was formerly a ducal residence and later in the 19th century the seat of the kings of Denmark. The fame of the Hanseatic Yachting School has spread far beyond the town itself.

Rendsburg gilt wegen seiner zentralen Lage als „Mittelpunkt" des Landes. Zentrum der Stadt bildet der Paradeplatz, in dessen Nähe sich die schönsten erhaltenen Gebäude befinden, wie zum Beispiel das Arsenal.
Alte und neue Baukunst vereinen sich zu einem harmonischen Stadtbild.

Rendsburg, largely because of its central position is the focal point of this region. The Paradeplatz is the centre of the town, in its immediate vicinity the most beautiful restored buildings can be seen, one of which is the Arsenal. Old and new houses together create a harmonious impression within the town.

Bereits im 18. Jahrhundert war Rendsburg mit Kiel durch den Bau eines Kanal verbunden. Mit dem Bau des Nord-Ostsee-Kanals erhielt Rendsburg die verkehrsmäßigen Voraussetzungen für seine Industrie, vor allem die Werften. Ein Wahrzeichen der Stadt ist die für den Eisenbahnverkehr gebaute Hochbrücke, die wegen der zusätzlich an ihr fahrenden Schwebefähre wohl einzigartig ist.

The construction of a canal in the 18th century created the link between Rendsburg and Kiel. The building of the Kiel Canal provided Rendsburg with the necessary traffic network for its industrial development, especially shipbuilding. A landmark of the town is the rail bridge which, as a unique feature, functions together with a hover ferry.

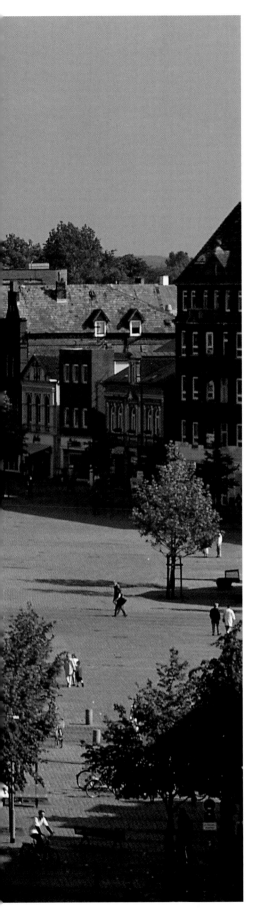

Bedingt durch die zentrale Lage ist Neumünster von jeher durch Handel und Gewerbe geprägt. Leder- und Tuchindustrie waren weit über die Landesgrenzen hinaus bekannt. Eine aktiv betriebene Unternehmensansiedlung glich den Rückgang dieser Wirtschaftszweige in den sechziger Jahren aus.

Neumünster ist auch heute noch bedeutendes Wirtschaftszentrum, Verkehrsknotenpunkt und Messestandort. Mitten in der Stadt gelegen, ist der Großflecken zentraler Marktplatz und Geschäftszentrum.

Neumünster's trade and commerce since its founding have been favourably influenced because of its central position. Its leather and textile industries have made it famous well beyond its borders. In the sixties new industries were encouraged to establish themselves as a counterbalance to the declining traditional industries. Today Neumünster is still an important centre of commerce, traffic junction and a location for trade fairs. In the middle of the town is the Grossflecken, the market and commercial hub of this thriving area.

Sehenswert bei einem Spaziergang durch die Stadt ist die Vicelinkirche, die 1834 fertiggestellt wurde und ein beachtliches Baudenkmal des norddeutschen Klassizismus darstellt.

Well worth a visit, during a stroll through the town, is the Vicelin church, completed in 1834, a notable example of the north German classical period.

Durch Neumünster fließt die
Schwale. Die Grünanlagen, die sie
begleiten, und der Teich in der
Stadtmitte laden zum Verweilen
ein.

*The river Schwale flows through
Neumünster. The green areas
adjacent to the banks of the river,
together with the pond in the
centre of the town are popular
meeting places.*

Das spätklassizistische Ständehaus in Itzehoe gilt als Geburtsstätte des Parlamentarismus in Schleswig-Holstein. Noch heute tagt hier die Ratsversammlung der Stadt. Es steht neben dem historischen Rathaus, das Ende des 17. Jahrhundert erbaut wurde. Der Turm der Laurentii-Kirche überragt die idyllische Atmosphäre der Innenstadt. Tradition und Fortschritt liegen hier nahe beieinander, das beweist das

Frauenhofer-Institut für Siliziumtechnologie (ISiT) nahe dem IZET, einem Innovationszentrum, das seit 1997 als Technologie- und Gründerzentrum dient.

The Ständehaus in Itzehoe, built in the late classical style, is recognised as the birthplace of the parliamentary system of Schleswig-Holstein. The building is still used for meetings of the town council. It is situated next to the historical town hall, erected at the end of the 17th century. The idyllic atmosphere of the town centre is dominated by the tower of the Laurentii church.

Tradition and progress exist here side by side. Evidence of this is the „Frauenhofer-Institut für Siliziumtechnologie" (ISiT) close to the IZET, a centre of innovation and since 1997 a technology and foundation centre.

Glückstadt, direkt an der Elbe gelegen, war 200 Jahre lang Ausgangs-
hafen der Walfangschiffe auf dem
Weg ins Eismeer. Durch den frucht-
baren Marschboden, der die Stadt
umgibt, entstand hier ein wichtiger
Umschlagsplatz für alle landwirt-
schaftlichen Produkte. In der Stadt
hinter den Elbdeichen befinden
sich bezaubernde Bürgerhäuser.

*Glückstadt on the river Elbe was
for 200 years the home port of the
whaling ships that sailed the polar
seas. The town became an
important trading place for
agricultural produce due to the
surrounding fertile marshland soil.
Behind the dykes on the river Elbe
can be seen enchanting period
houses.*

Heide, Verwaltungssitz des Landkreises Dithmarschen, ist stolz auf seinen Marktplatz, der mit einer Größe von 4,7 Hektar als der größte der Bundesrepublik gilt. Er diente als Versammlungsort der mittelalterlichen Bauernrepublik. Seit dem 17. Jahrhundert steht die St.-Jürgen Kirche in ihrer jetzigen Form auf diesem Platz.

Heide, the administrative seat of the district of Dithmarschen, is proud of its spacious market place, with an area of 4.7 hectares it is the largest in the Federal Republic. It also served as a place of assembly during the medieval peasants` republic. The St. Jürgen church in its present form has stood on this square since the 17th century.

Die Kulturspuren der ersten Besiedlung Schleswig-Holsteins sind noch vielerorts zu erkennen. Wie diese beiden Großsteingräber nahe Albersdorf und Schwabstedt sind noch etwa 300 weitere erhalten. Es waren wohl Sippengräber der führenden sozialen Schicht. Große, im Kreis aufgestellte Findlinge wurden nach oben mit Deckensteinen verschlossen und meist zu Hügeln aufgeschüttet. Im Laufe der Zeit haben Regen und Wind die lockere Erde abgetragen, so daß die großen Steine (Megalithen) wieder sichtbar werden.

Traces of early settlements in Schleswig-Holstein are to be found in many places. Besides the two megalithic graves in the vicinity of Albersdorf and Schwabstedt, a further 300 have been preserved. Presumably whole clans of the upper social strata were buried in these graves. Large boulders positioned in a circle covered with stone slabs were then piled with earth in the shape of mounds. With the passage of time, rain and wind have swept away the earth, leaving the megalithic stones exposed as monuments.

Das uralte Spiel der Gezeiten hat die Menschen der Westküste häufig in Atem gehalten. Das Eidersperrwerk wehrt seit 1973 Schäden für Land und Leute ab. Fünf Segmenttore verhindern das Eindringen der Nordsee bei Flut. Bei Ebbe werden sie wieder geöffnet, um das dann gestaute Wasser der Eider abfließen zu lassen.

From time immemorial the everchanging drama of the tides has held the people of the west coast in awe, however, since 1973 the Eider Dam has provided protection against damage for land and population. The five individual gates prevent the penetration of the North Sea during a flood. At low tide the gates are opened allowing the collected water to flow back into the river Eider.

Die Büsumer Krabbenkutter prägen noch immer das Bild des Hafens und sind attraktives Ziel der vielen Urlaubsgäste, die den Badeort besuchen.

The prawn boats still provide a picturesque scene at Büsum's harbour and are an attraction for many of the holidaymakers visiting the seaside resort.

Im Küstenbereich, dem nur zeit-
weise überfluteten Vorland, bieten
die Salzwiesen einen wertvollen
Lebensraum für rund 2000 Tier-
und Pflanzenarten.

Der Herrensitz Hoyerswort war
einst Sitz des Statthalters auf Eiderstedt, dessen angegliederte Scheune
die typischen Merkmale eines Hau-
barges ausweist. Diese, normaler-
weise auch als Wohnhaus genutzten
Wirtschaftsgebäude, beeindrucken
durch ihre stattliche Größe.

*In the coastal regions the salt
meadows of the temporarily
flooded shore areas provide an
important habitat for approximately
2000 species of animal and plant
life. The manor house at
Hoyerswort with its attached barn
was once the seat of the governor
of Eiderstedt. The barn has the
typical features of an early
farmhouse. These farm-buildings
then normally used as living
quarters, are impressive because of
their enormous size.*

Auf der breiten Sandbank vor St. Peter-Ording sind Pfahlbauten eine unverwechselbare Attraktion. Auf diese Weise vor Sturmfluten geschützt, bieten sie den Badegästen Versorgung an dem weiten Strand. Auch im Winter bewahrt er seinen Reiz und lockt die Spaziergänger.

A unique attraction on the sandbank outside St. Peter-Ording are the houses on stilts. Protected from flooding they provide facilities for the many holidaymakers using the wide stretch of the beach. Even in winter this resort retains its charms and is an attraction for many walkers.

Der ewige Wechsel der Gezeiten beherrscht diese Küste. Alle sechs Stunden lösen Ebbe und Flut einander ab. Wegen der Einzigartigkeit dieses Naturraumes und zu seinem Erhalt hat man dieses Gebiet zum Nationalpark Schleswig-Holsteinisches Wattenmeer erklärt.

Der rot-weiße Leuchtturm von Westerhever, seit 1907 weit draußen auf einer Warft in Betrieb, wirkt so malerisch, daß er häufig als Werbesymbol für Schleswig-Holstein verwendet wird.

The everchanging tides dominate this part of the coast. Low and high tides change every six hours. Because of its unique character and for its protection this area was declared the Nature Park Schleswig-Holsteinisches Wattenmeer (mudflats).

The red and white lighthouse of Westerhever, far out to sea on a promontory, has been in operation since 1907. It is often used as an advertising symbol for Schleswig-Holstein because it is so picturesque.

Friedrichstadt ist ein architektonisches Schmuckstück. Bei einem Spaziergang entlang der baumgesäumten Grachten könnte man meinen, in eine niederländiche Kleinstadt versetzt zu sein. Dies kommt nicht von ungefähr, denn holländische Glaubensflüchtlinge bauten einst diese Stadt, die immer als Freistätte für viele verschiedene Religiongemeinschaften galt.

Friedrichstadt is a preserved architectural jewel. Walking along the tree-lined "Grachten" one can easily imagine oneself in a small Dutch town, not without reason, for this town was originally built by Dutch religious refugees and has always been a sanctuary for many different religious communities.

Für alle Zeit wird der Stadt anhängen, was ihr berühmtester Sohn in einem Gedicht schrieb: Theodor Storm (1817-1888) brachte Husum in den Ruf, „graue Stadt am Meer" zu sein. Aber wenn im Frühjahr Tausende von Krokussen im Schloßpark blühen, trifft diese Aussage nicht mehr zu.

Husum will retain for all time the description that its most famous son Theodor Storm (1817-1888) wrote about it, hence the reputation "the grey town by the sea". Even though in spring thousands of crocusses flower in the castle grounds, this unfair description still remains.

Besonders im Marktbereich zeugen viele Bauten von den Glanzzeiten Husums. Einen Kontrast dazu bietet das moderne Rathaus, das sich, direkt am Hafen gelegen, architektonisch einer Bootshalle anlehnt.

Around the market place many fine buildings are to be seen, relics from its heyday as an important port. In contrast to these period houses stands the modern town hall situated directly on the harbour which architecturally resembles a boathouse.

Der stetig wechselnde Ausdruck der Landschaft durch die elementaren Kräfte von Wind und Wasser hat den Expressionisten Emil Nolde (1867-1956) immer beschäftigt. Seine farbenprächtigen und unverwechselbaren Landschaftsbilder dokumentieren dies. Sein Haus in Seebüll dient heute als Museum. Viele seiner Blumenbilder hat er dort in seinem Garten gemalt.

The everchanging mood of the landscape created by the elements of wind and water was a constant inspiration to the expressionist painter Emil Nolde (1867-1956). His colourful and distinctive landscape paintings are evidence of this. His house in Seebüll is now a museum. Many of his flower paintings were painted in his own garden.

Seit 1634 fuhren die Amrumer auf holländischen Walfangschiffen in das Nordmeer. Häufig als Kapitäne und Steuerleute, wie man es auf den sehenswerten Grabsteinen lesen kann. Als der Walfang nichts mehr einbrachte, wanderten viele aus und suchten ihr Glück in Amerika. Viele der reetgedeckten Friesenhäusern sind zu beliebten Urlaubsunterkünften geworden. Der Leuchturm von Amrum ist der höchste der deutschen Nordseeküste und mit seiner Reichweite von gut 40km eine wichtige Orientierungsmarke für die Schiffahrt.

Since 1634 Amrum's sailors have sailed as crew members on Dutch whaling ships into the Arctic Sea, often as captains and helmsmen which can be verified from their handsome tombstones. After whaling was no longer profitable, many of these mariners emigrated to America to seek their fortune. Most of the thatched Friesian-style houses have become sought-after accommodation for holidaymakers. Amrum's lighthouse is the highest on the North Sea coast and with a range of 40 kms is an important guide for shipping.

Wyk auf Föhr ist das älteste Seebad an der Westküste. Schon 1819 erkannten die Föhrer, daß man auch andere Erwerbswege als die der Seefahrt nutzen mußte. Man erreicht die Insel mit den Fähren der Wyker-Dampfschiffs-Reederei. Föhr wird zu Recht die „Grüne Insel" genannt.

Wyk on the island of Föhr is the oldest seaside resort on the west coast. As early as 1819 the inhabitants of Föhr realised that there were other sources of income apart from seafaring. The island can be reached with ferries of the Wyker Dampfschiffs-Reederei. Föhr is quite rightly known as the "Green Island".

Sylt ist seit 1927 durch den Hinden-
burgdamm mit dem Festland verbunden. Die Insel besticht durch
eine einmalige Küstenlandschaft.
Angesichts einer beschaulichen
Abendstimmung am Strand ist es
kaum vorstellbar, daß bei Sturm
die Wellen der Nordsee mit einer
Höhe von bis zu 17 Metern auf
den Strand schlagen.

*In 1927 the Hindenburg Causeway
linking Sylt to the mainland was
built. The island is famous for its
unique and beautiful coastline. It is
hard to imagine when enjoying
such a tranquil end-of-the-day
atmosphere on the beach that it
can be the scene of storms with
waves from the North Sea up to 17
metres high pounding that same
beach.*

In dem exklusiven Badeort Westerland auf Sylt geht es schon beinah
großstädtisch zu. Im Kontrast dazu
stehen die beschaulich gehaltenen
Orte der Insel, in denen der frie-
sische Baustil noch sehr gepflegt
wird. So auch in Wenningstedt, wo
eine Tür am Hause eines Walfängers
vom Wohlstand seiner Bewohner
kündet.

*In Sylt's capital, the exclusive
seaside resort of Westerland, one
almost has the feeling of being in
urban surroundings. In contrast to
which are situated the charming,
preserved places on the island
where the Friesian-style of building
is very much maintained. A good
example is Wenningstedt, where
the door of a house belonging to a
whaler would bear witness to the
prosperity of the owner.*

93

Helgoland, die einzige deutsche Hochseeinsel, sticht mit ihren unverwechselbaren roten Felsen aus der dunklen See hervor. Der knapp 50m hohe Felsturm, „Lange Anna" genannt, gilt als ihr Wahrzeichen. Die autofreie Insel ist noch nicht einmal 1km² groß. Ihr Schicksal schien beinah besiegelt, als im April 1947 6000t Munition zur Explosion gebracht wurden. Durch das gesunde Hochseeklima und das Privileg der Zollfreiheit ist Helgoland wieder beliebtes Urlaubs- und Ausflugsziel geworden.

Heligoland is the only German island on the open sea, dramatic with its unmistakeable red rock standing out of the dark waters. The tall rock called "Lange Anna", almost 50 metres high, is the landmark of the island. The traffic-free island with an area of less than 1 square kilometre almost met its end when in April 1947 6,000 tons of ammunition were exploded. Since then Heligoland has once again become a popular destination for both holidaymakers and day-trippers, largely because of its healthy sea air and duty-free privileges.

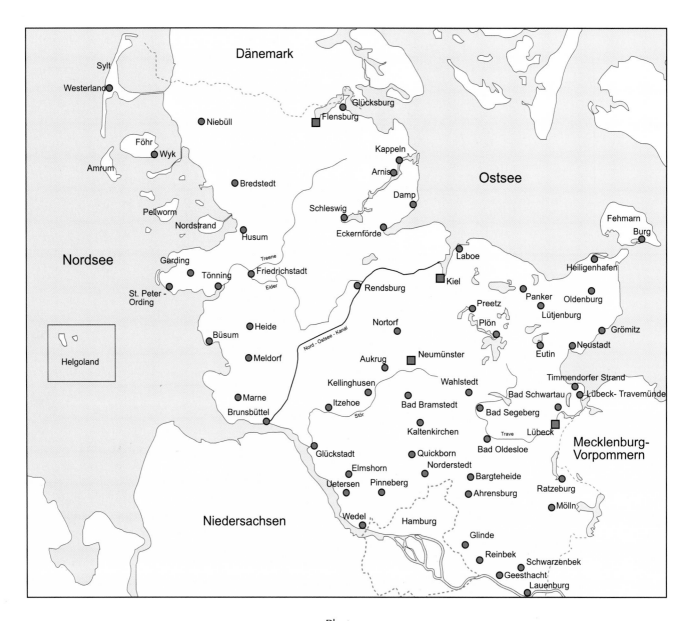

Photos:

Dieter Steffen, Hamburg
Uwe Paulsen, Neumünster

Archäologisches Landesmuseum, Schleswig
Photo dpa: Laboe
Martin Eichhorn, Haseleu
Kurverwaltung Helgoland
mp-press-helgoland
Udo Karstens, Neumünster

Übersetzung: Margret Brown FIL

ISBN 3-529-05323-6